Scribbled Lines: Life in Pieces

Scribbled Lines: Life in Pieces

Poems by

Michael A. Roberts

© 2023 Michael A. Roberts. All rights reserved.
This material may not be reproduced in any form, published,
reprinted, recorded, performed, broadcast,
rewritten or redistributed without
the explicit permission of Michael A. Roberts.
All such actions are strictly prohibited by law.

Cover design by Shay Culligan
Cover photo by Ire Creative

ISBN: 978-1-63980-276-0

Kelsay Books
502 South 1040 East, A-119
American Fork, Utah 84003
Kelsaybooks.com

I would like to dedicate this collection to my daughters, Cayce and Kathryn, for being the sources of deep and eternal inspiration; to Bruce and Mom, who left too early but left inspiring memories; to Dan and Steven for their support; and to Angela, for being so patient and enduring the sometimes-challenging life of living with a writer

Contents

I. Random Roadside Cemetery

Random Roadside Cemetery	15
In the Fall	16
The Last Song	17
The Crooked Path	18
Apocalypse Now	19
Bricks	20
Atheists' Prayer	21
Windshine	22
The Tavern	23
Drinker	24
A Good Day	25
Choices	26
Reflection	27
Shadows	28
Legacy	29
Colors	30
Hourglass	31
Replacements	32
Rehearsal	33
Mortality	34

II. Resurrection on the River

Riptide	37
Turtles	38
Compromise with the Rain	39
Warthog	40
Poodles	41
Grasslands	42
Sunlight	43
Advice from birds	44

Another Path	45
Killer Frost	46
The River	47
Rocks	48
Stargazer	49
The Leaf	50
Wisdom	51
Raging River	52
Sunbursts	53

III. The Unstable Hourglass

Two	57
Butterfly (Kathryn)	58
New Life (Cayce)	59
Coffee	60
Departure	61
Figure skater	62
Proposal	63
Companions	64
Pittsburgh	65
Bubbles	66
Post-Traumatic Stress	67
Paper Roses	68
Flowers at the Airport	69
For Mom	70
Clouds	71
Volcano	72
The Book	73
Dark Angel	74
The Last Time	75
The Solitary Palm	76
Night Sweats	77

Pieces of me	78
Goals	79
Dark Lady	80
Life of my time	81
Insomnia 2	82
Stay with me	83
Morning Coffee	84
The Butterfly and the Unicorn	85
Phoenix	86
The Dance	87
The Getaway	88
The End	89
The End II	90

IV. Redundant Ambiguity

Haunted Jail	93
Shattered	94
Lethargy	95
Hopscotch	96
Coins	97
November	98
Change	99
A Dollar	100
Faith	101
The Judge	102
Hands	103
The Candle	104
Grief	105
Regrets	106
The Path	107
Happy Hour	108
Pittsburgh	109

Writer's Block	110
Authors I know	111
Silence	112
The Sandbox	113
Escorts	114
The Kathryn Doctrine	115
Everyone is a poet	116
Fountain	117
Annulment	118
The Song	119
Luggage	120
At Sunrise	121
Intermission	122
Insomnia	123
Cyborg	124
The Couch	125
Soulmates	126
The Fortress	127
The Sword	128
Reapers	129
Dancing Scarecrow	130
The Book of Me	131
Currents	132
The House Across the Street	133
Aspirations	134
Baptism	135
"Woke" Barbie	136
Facebook	137
Jack-in-the-box	138
Where do I go?	139

I.
Random Roadside Cemetery

Random Roadside Cemetery

A life that's lost, a soul that's found,
Memories slumber underground

On a country roadside all alone,
Faded words on dusty stone

Weathered plastic flowers fade,
The end of life's masquerade

No name of church or family
Roadside anonymity

When they came and when they went,
Epitaph enlightenment

A family of stone to catch the eye
Of random autos passing by

In the Fall

In the Fall of our mortality,
In the uncluttering of our reflections and regrets,
That procrastinating reality
Knocks on our door to collect its debts.

The middle-aged discontent
Is replaced with desperate fires.
We rationalize and canonize endeavors spent
For the perfunctory consumption of feckless desires.

In the winter of our inconsequence,
The orgy of despondence and recompense
Consumes the trivial habitual ambivalence
In our paramount dissention with providence . . .

The Last Song

The pensive piano performing in life's background
Is only conspicuously played when disconsolate moments
And incriminated regrets suspend our neglectful streams of
consciousness.

It is the soundtrack of contrition and lamentation,
The theme of discontent and despondency,
The rhythm of disillusionment and compunction . . .

When our ears have been stripped of the discordant cacophony of
life and breathing,
We hear above the solemnity of sacrament and commendatory
rhetoric and weeping . . .
The accompanying keys being perceptibly struck as the piano
plays us off the stage of life.

The Crooked Path

The path continues somewhere over the hills,
dodging trees and rays of setting sunlight,
and is only visible a shadowed measure at a time.
It compels us to investigate the mystery of its destination,
The gamble of heartbreak and glory . . .
A solitary path, a lone pursuer
of promises hidden in the unseen horizon . . .
A promise of a trace of morning beyond the nighttime

Apocalypse Now

If the world ends tomorrow,
I am positive that I shall ride out the sunset
of nuclear showers of disappointment and grievance
by blazing a torrent of radioactive profanities to the orange
heavens
and defiantly displaying two prominent middle digits
lifted at the pretend overseer in masturbatory reverence

Bricks

Crawling, we build our brick foundation
for our interactions with our environment.
Walking, we add the windows
Through which we see the world.
Running, we open the doors
To relationships.
Driving, we travel the world,
exploring the wonder of possibilities.
Working, we establish our place in the world
our names, our reputations, our influence . . .
Understanding, we build a moat between ourselves and the world,
And set it on fire . . .

Atheists' Prayer

Dear Lord,
who does not exist,
Please hear my prayer,
in which I do not believe,
So that I may not suffer
in hell fire damnation
That is just a myth
of the weak and needy—
Amen

Windshine

The paucity of sunshine may discourage some.
They require its rays of validation to affirm feeling
Its luminosity offers recompense and solace.
Its warmth provides reimbursement for sentences served
Under deflating emotional clouds and unnerving thunderstorms.

I have an affinity for the adulterer-the wind . . .
Its affair with the rain delivers an atmospheric baptism
That floods my senses and restores my soul.
The wind's tryst with the snowfall stalls commotion
And allows me to reflect thoughts beside still waters.

The wind frolics with the frost, and the cool breath of winter
Sweeps across the shadowed valley of discontent,
Rejuvenating and anointing me with a righteous purpose.
Still, the wind will occasionally fornicate with the sun,
Shepherding my spirit across the green pastures of eternity.

The Tavern

There is a tavern for guys like me
where the regulars and the bartenders
know our names
and our stories
and give us credit
not for who they know us to be
but for the legends
they know that we wish to be

Drinker

"What I'm telling me," he said,
"Is I need a drink to clear my head.
She had lots of good reasons for leaving.
I've got pints and pints here for grieving.
I really don't like my job that much,
So I use a shot as a sort of crutch.
My kids don't call to check on me.
Vodka helps to set me free.
That I'm unhappy is no surprise,
Or my fondness for tequila sunrise.
My health is poor because I'm old,
But whiskey makes me feel more bold.
I sit at this bar just full of doubt.
So many things to drink about."

A Good Day

I sat on the bank of a dark, deep lake
Throwing stones as my thoughts juggled the twin losses of spirit
and will . . .
An ant broke my mediation and said,
"It's a good day to die.
Winter will come soon and chill the blood in our veins
And stop a frozen heart whose beat has already slowed . . ."
"It's a good day to die," added the butterfly
"The wind is building and will soon cover us with the dust
And ashes and cinders from the desires we abandoned with our
hope . . ."
"It is, indeed, a good day to die," said the grasshopper.
The clouds are starting to gather and darken,
And they will block the light from any promise we have been
owed . . ."
"It's a good day to die . . . today . . ." said the frog
"The rain will come and the immense flood of disappointment
And disillusionment will drown our dreams and ambitions . . ."
"I was thinking of the fire," I said,
"And the belief it consumes, the expectations it forsakes, and all
the faith it singes . . ."
And just then, the ripples in the water from the stones
Were just beginning to reach the shore . . .

Choices

No one would look up at a rainbow of black,
No one would dip in an ocean of grey.
No one would reach for a ring made of iron,
No one would welcome a cloudy day

No one would pray if there wasn't a heaven,
No one would laugh if it only brought tears,
No one would bother to give a heart that was broken,
No one would trade me for my older years

No one would welcome night without sleep,
No one would smile if it only showed sorrow,
No one would choose to write instead of live,
No one would choose one great last day over another tomorrow

Reflection

I reached the top
right here at the bottom.
I lived a colorful life
that was much too grey.
The present has arrived
entirely too late.
The straight road here
was full of twists and turns.
Time passed by slowly
ever so quickly.
I learned a lot about me
From the stranger in the mirror

Shadows

My shadow follows and mimics me,
employing the landscape for a dark canvas,
bending and re-shaping in a way I am incapable . . .
He uses imperceptibility as a strategy
to hide the evidence that would disclose
our intertwined soul and destiny . . .
We are unified and demarcated
As I seek redemption from the sky,
and he struggles to sustain my presence
between him and the light

Legacy

I sat in the back pew
observing the black somber parade
of those who honored or regarded me in life.
The real gift we have when we have a heartbeat
is to imbed a seed that blossoms at our demise
to impart wisdom someone will recall after we depart
to leave a moment of laughter that spontaneously ignites
to move someone in some way that we leave more
than just perpetual DNA
and a legacy of temporary tears

Colors

White—and the frenzied blur of sensations and expectations,
Green—and the impetuous discovery and adventure of endeavors and experience,
Red—and the exuberant passion and vigor of pursuit and conquest,
Yellow—and the inevitable interruption of hesitation and reflection,
Blue—and the idiomatic melancholy of regret and reappraisal retrospect,
Brown—and the desolate dissolution of cognition and corporeal concomitant,
Grey—and despondent anticipation of repose and nihilism,
Then black . . .

Hourglass

Nearly imperceptible in their rush to finality,
The grains of sand submit to gravity and
Fling themselves impulsively and impetuously
Toward a determined and conspicuous fate.
Consolidating with those who proceeded the Fall,
Gazing up at the height from which the tumble originated,
The epiphany of meaning strikes—
It was on the precipice that their existence was robust, integral . . .
That immeasurable, imperceptible moment of stasis before launch
From finite to the infinite.

Replacements

Caffeine replaces morning energy,
Glasses instead of eyes to see,
Computer profiles replace my friends,
Receding hairline replacing split ends,
Short walks in the afternoon instead of a morning run,
An SUV instead of muscle car fun . . .
Now "well-done" is replaced with "well-said,"
Each daughter's clean, neat room, and empty bed . . .

Rehearsal

What is hot and what is fire?
Which is whim and which desire?
Which is love and which is lust?
Who to avoid and who to trust?
When to go and when to stay?
Who'll be loyal and who will betray?
When to bet and when to fold?
What is rich and what's fools' gold?
What makes a hero or a fool?
When will desire start to cool?
Which is luck and which is curse?
Life never let me rehearse.

Mortality

The surest symptoms
of a wasted life
are
breathing,
a pulse,
and thinking

II.

Resurrection on the River

Riptide

The cinematic curl of the wave charms and beguiles the swimmers
who ride the majestic water steed from the sharks to the minnows . . .
The force of the wave rising from the ocean thrills the boarders
who rip along its chicane in a synchronous aquatic ballet . . .

The rhythm of the wave lures the white-winged sea gulls
who hover above the churning tide to pluck out their disoriented meals . . .
The allure of the wave seduces the tormented
who gather for the therapeutic rolling symphony of peace

But it is the shore that experiences the scathing indignation of the wave
as she unremorsefully strips away the dignity of her closest companion . . .
By striking and withdrawing the lash, she peels away layer after layer
faith and conviction eroded by the surf

Turtles

There comes a moment at the end of every day
when the turtles gather under a setting sun
by the pond's shore,
And, ignoring the flurry of the fish
and the dominion of the ducks,
Make ripples in the water
As they poke their heads
to the surface
to observe the old man casting the breadcrumbs
of his life into the water

Compromise with the Rain

The problem with the rain is not the wet,
It is the companionship of his brother, thunder
And his sister, lightning . . .
The deluge drowns hopes and wishes and prayers,
And the pounding drums and streaking light
Add unnecessary reinforcement to the capricious
whims and will of the impetuous clouds.
They can drive our lives far away.
But the passing of the showers
and the cessation of rumbling and flashing
are no guarantees that golden rays will shine
on our life after . . .
No slow warming or casual temperate embrace
back from the cloudburst assault . . .
Sometimes sunshine is too much to ask,
and we may be content with the absence of storms

Warthog

My spirit animal is the warthog . . .
He is unapologetically a hog
With warts exposed to the world . . .
True to his own nature,
Aesthetically repulsive,
Invulnerable to criticism,
An impenetrable sense of self-worth,
Defying conformity and ubiquitous demands
For compliance and compromise

Poodles

Shaking never releases the leg-humping poodle . . .
One must vigorously and manifestly swat the tempestuous fornicator,
And then kick without contrition at the air of its retreating rump
Because there are days we need to send the unwavering message
That we are just tired of being fucked with

Grasslands

The imposition of conscience and morality
wounds and hobbles the righteous
on life's savanna . . .
The instinct of courtesy and congeniality
expose the vulnerable impalas
to the bone-crushing experience
of the nihilistic cheetahs

Sunlight

The coldest beam of light
is that narrowest sliver
that shines the sun on possibility
just long enough to entice you
into a thunderstorm

Advice from birds

"There is much to see in the world,"
said the cardinal,
Before being blindsided by the kid's pellet . . .
"There is much in the world to believe,"
said the blue jay,
Before returning to her nest of molested eggs . . .
"There is much in the world to rejoice over,"
said the robin,
Before meeting his fate against the windshield of the Range Rover . . .
"There is much in the world to consider,"
said the woodpecker,
Before the lightning bolt terminated his cognition . . .
"There is much in the world to fear,"
said the vulture,
Feasting on the remains of my corpse
While the owl looked away.

Another Path

The goose waddled beside me and said,
"There is no straight path between here and the barn.
If willing, you will have to veer from the usual path
and fight your way through a dense wood
avoiding poisonous serpents and spiders to reach it."
At the barn, I encountered a horse.
"There is no straight path from here to the meadow," he said.
"If willing, you will have to trudge through the deep mud,
avoiding being trampled by a raging bull and swarming hornets."
At the meadow, I encountered a doe who said,
"There is no straight path from here to the mountain. If willing,
you must avoid the flooding river tide and jump trail to trail until
you reach the base."
At the base of the mountain, I found the Lamb.
The Lamb said to me, "Now that you have found me,
the path is straight from here to salvation."

Killer Frost

A lonely pine on the edge of the wood line,
demarcated from the dense forest,
Stands stooped, gazing at the frozen carpet below.
It is weighed down by an unsuspecting frost
which now leaves it hovering in desperation and anguish.
The pine's present predicament does no justice
to the profile of the burgeoning evergreen
Standing stoutly and defiantly, for a time,
against the cutting wind and chilling rain—
Optimistic, bold, and full of promise,
Stretching toward the dawn each morning,
Claiming victory season over season . . .
Until the moonless night
Gave cover to the frigid assassin
Who assaulted the vulnerable pine,
stripped it of its dignity and pride,
Robbed it of its essence,
And slipped away before the sunrise—
leaving the skeletal remains
of a lonely, broken sap

The River

Dragonflies hover effortlessly over the quiet and serene current,
Petals from surrounding trees helicopter and land silently on the rushing water,
An occasional fish breaches the exterior to catch a moment of the setting sun.
The only sound is the water scampering over rocks and fallen trees from the shoreline.
The trees bend to the banks to marvel at their own reflections.
A breeze sweeps over the current,
Waltzing with the grass and shrubs that decorate the landscape,
Bidding good evening to all the creatures that gather nearby . . .
And a dark burden from above
violently pierces the surface and settles
beneath the shadow of the bridge

Rocks

As a boy, I stood on the bumpy and dusty bank of a hidden pond
Camouflaged by tall trees, overgrown bushes, and a militia of weeds,
tightly gripping a menacing stone that lacked only a target.
I waited with atypical patient focus for a turtle, beaver, frog,
or other prey to show themselves and become the victim of my accuracy and lust.
As my heels sank into the brown mush surrounding the pond,
Unexpectedly, an unsuspecting mallard appeared at the border of the water,
Arriving for his penance of flagellation . . .
Cocking my arm, I picked a precise, surely fatal mark on his head . . .
But he turned, and looked, as if to accept his sacrificial fate.
I froze, then began to shake, and then to cry.
Because I was not without sin, I dropped the rock in the muddy footprint of my escape.
As the sun was dropping, I walked home along a dusty road lined on both sides with pebbles, stones, and boulders.

Stargazer

Stargazing is an appropriate
metaphor for human nature.
While we make wishes
on faraway twinkling bodies
and marvel at the majesty
and wonder and proportion
of God's universe,
we are unaware
of the cataclysmic
meteor
that lies hidden
behind the distraction
of the stars
of contentment

The Leaf

The leaf departs from the security of its home
At the insistence of the wind . . .
It departs tentatively
And floats lively on the swirling breeze,
Finally settling on the subtle current
Of the river,
Drifting aimless toward an unknown destiny

Wisdom

Chasing the wind-blown petals of a dandelion
beneath gathering gray clouds
across a vast brown fall meadow,
I encountered a solitary, stationary squirrel . . .
He, at me, stared
And I, of him, asked shyly,
"What is the secret of life?"
"Nuts," he said,
And scampered up a tree,
Leaving me to be mocked by the woodpecker

Raging River

The sound of rain on the river
Is how defeat would sound if it were a noise . . .
The crashing of water against itself,
Like a liquid shadow or echo,
The current and downpour
Both futile attempts to escape themselves,
Their nature, their essence, their destiny . . .
The redundant ubiquity
In a cycle of vain attempts
At reinvention, reimagination,
An unconscious resignation of conformity
To an original designated essence . . .

Sunbursts

The molten sun dissolves into a distant horizon,
The residual sunbursts cascade down to Earth
With a meandering curiosity,
Oblivious of their own luminosity,
A brilliance of golden confetti
To blanket a darkening world
With a temporary luminescence
To brighten the world
Before the apocalypse

III.

The Unstable Hourglass

Two

There will be two blades of grass sustained green
in the vast perishing brown meadow—
two that continue the memory of the flourishing spring
against the pallet of brown carpet surrounding the subsiding fall
lake . . .
There will be two rays of sunlight creeping across a window
as the sun bows in the day's finale in the winter sky—
two radiant twinkles of light that dance in the dark hallway
of an abandoned home darkened by the retreating sun . . .
There will be two brilliant stars maintaining majesty
and occupying and opposing the onyx consummation—
two unambiguous resplendent lanterns
persevering in the darkened canopy of the moonless night . . .
There will be two leaves left dancing on a bare limb
of a river birch seized by an oppressive winter wind—
two exultant sprouts that celebrate,
And there will be two hearts that continue to beat
behind the two shadows cast against the diminished sunlight,
two heads bowed in appreciation and reverence
to a headstone of granite and letters paying tribute to mortality

Butterfly (Kathryn)

I am awed by the way a breeze lifts you so freely
and you surf the chicane of the wind
as your kaleidoscope wings bring color to a pale world.
You giggle as you tiptoe playfully across the grass,
your wings letting you lightly touch each blade,
delicate and memorable.
Your path through life is arbitrary
and your arrival spreads contagious laughter
where you choose to briefly settle.
You embrace a gypsy spirit and bohemian cadence,
ignoring expectation for endless possibilities,
conforming only to the rhythm of your own free spirit.
The caterpillar has grown, and changed, and blossomed
and has all too soon and much too eagerly
left the cocoon of her father's lap

New Life (Cayce)

I lost my breath as you gasped for air,
I lost touch with what was real as you became aware,
I cried on the inside as you cried for all to hear,
They wiped your eyes, I wiped a tear,
A splendid candlelight, a fading flame,
You felt scared, I felt the same,
You held on tight, I kept control,
You smiled at me and restored a soul

Coffee

There is a sort of caffeinated bravery in the morning
that consummates with a poverty of will
And a sort of imposition of anxiety,
Delivered from expectations of imagined interconnection,
That, again, places me firmly, but awkwardly, leaning in your doorway,
Coupling manufactured courage with manifest cowardice,
Repeating this silent, sad melody of suicide and sanguineness—
A futile ritual proposal of an ambivalent scarecrow

Departure

The sliver of morning sun that travels lazily across our bed
will agitate the deep repose of the angelic denizen
who peacefully occupies the hollow space between my chest and heart
and will summon her to vacate our asylum
for the commitments of a selfish and heedless world
and leave me in an invariable misty melancholy,
reminiscing, nostalgic
for the divine magic of my face in her hair

Figure skater

Power and grace twirling and spinning,
A flair of theatrics in a world of ice . . .
Blades gracefully shred the frozen pallet,
Her dance is her animated soul—
Furious and elegant . . .
Here, the adrenaline pulses and her heart erupts,
She finds salvation on thin twin blades
That she cannot wear onto
The rink of life

Proposal

Lie and accept what you cannot take,
Lie and offer what you cannot give,
Lie and promise what you may betray,
Lie and plan a life that you cannot live,
Lie and affirm a question you may reject,
Lie with tears that will dry so soon
Deception has a voluntary fool,
On one knee, under this moon

Companions

Join me in the darkness,
Join me in the rain,
Join me in the melancholy,
Join me in the pain,
Join me for the heartache,
Join me for the tears,
Join me for the scarring,
That will last for years and years . . .
Join me in the lonely,
Be my partner in the fire,
Share with me the pain we feel
Losing our soul's desire

Pittsburgh

Cold and unforgiving,
Indifferent, unsympathetic
Hardened structural steel
Gray and uncaring
Harsh and callous
Strident and severe
A life rhythm of hammer on metal
Beating inside your chest
Somewhere in Pittsburgh

Bubbles

for Kathryn

With your heaviest inhale,
you puff your reddening cheeks
and blow with childish might
through the tiny plastic ring of soap
and marvel at the burgeoning
incandescent bubble
that will, like you one day,
lift and float elegantly away
on a capricious spring breeze.

Post-Traumatic Stress

A night of passion with a ghost of you,
Like a night of passion that we knew,
I touched the outline of your face,
But your mind was in another place.
I held you in silent candlelight,
With empty arms another night.
I caressed your body and stroked your hair,
Your worthless whispers in the air . . .
Making love to the promises you made,
The apparition starts to fade . . .
You raped my heart and ever since,
I cuddle with your indifference

Paper Roses

I followed you again today,
But never closed the distance . . .
The potential access to truth restrains me.
It comes with a stabbing pain . . .
My heart encumbers my feet.
I am not ready to surrender to the cinders . . .
And as the silent distance grows between us,
You never glance over your shoulder . . .
I am content in the shadows of ignorance
And the ambiguity of the summer rain,
Stalking the silhouette of who I thought you were

Flowers at the Airport

Open your eyes if you want to see the sun
breaching the cloud-strangled skyline
at dawn,
Spread your arms if you want to feel the refreshing wind
stir and renew the leaf-littered landscape
of fall,
Stand up tall and inhale deeply if you want to taste the rain
conspiring in puddles beneath your feet
until spring,
Turn your head and listen carefully to hear the majestic waves
returning to shore with the proud thunder
of conquest
Or sit here with me curled with arms around our knees
eyes closed and desperately grappling with the evil spirits
of reflection

For Mom

I lie entombed also, but in an emotional sarcophagus . . .
A solitary cognitive journey from a boy holding your hand
To a man holding my breath . . .
Your passing is the ellipsis on my life,
An incomplete sentence left open by irretrievable words . . .
Unredeemed promises, and a forfeited future,
Reclusive in my recollections, a reminder of you
In the acoustic metallic sound of the spring breeze
lightly embracing the windchimes

Clouds

You,
my love,
are like the sun.
And now,
I need
the clouds
for shade . . .
fully aware
that the price
will most likely
be rain.

Volcano

The terror of volcanoes
is the unseen—
The mystery and anxiety
caused by the unknown and unexpected
Being, fermenting there,
hidden from our eyes
and defended against any prediction,
a level of rage and devastation
that will be capriciously triggered
by unknown factors and unjust causes . . .
Even as you stare at me peacefully
over your cup of morning coffee.

The Book

The book of you lies
undiscovered
in a dark corner
of a dark room
in a dark world
covered in a jacket of dust
with a rigid spine
and beautiful poetry
that cannot be read.

Dark Angel

I can distinguish the Dark Angel
from the Angel of Darkness . . .
The former will arrive after trial and torment,
Recounting with reproach my misdeeds and miscarriages,
Claiming payment for sins of hubris and transgressions . . .
Spawning oppressive reflective thought and regret,
Demanding penance . . .
The latter is the intrepid silhouette
Displayed seductively in my doorway,
The personification of temptation and desire
Penetrating the shadows and existential hindrances
To salvage my soul

The Last Time

Just let me listen . . .
Allow me to feel the whisps of your breath
Wash over my neck as you whisper to me . . .
Let my mind escape with your ideas,
As the echo of your giggles cascade over my body . . .
Let my eyes capture the incandescence of your smile
And sink into the depth of your gaze . . .
And indulge reflection of the dancing candlelight
Because this memory is the treasure I have
After not knowing yesterday
That you had no tomorrow . . .

The Solitary Palm

for Angela

A solitary palm tree
Is content to rest beneath the persistent warmth
of the congenial sun,
Thankful for the steadiness of the network
of roots that have securely
established its foundation in the fertile conditions
in its consecrated tropical domain,
Never disregarding or presupposing
its integral iconoclastic stature,
And never forsaking its tranquility
for a moment's consideration of transition or transformation—
until its soul is unsuspectingly grazed by the alluring kiss
and temptation of the enchanting and seductive zephyr.

Night Sweats

A quiet, secluded place,
An uneasy accord, a hidden face,
A deep remorse, a quiet pain,
Intently listening to the rain . . .
Unseen, unheard inside the dark,
Exclamation point and question mark,
A diminishing light from the other room,
An emotional corpse inside this tomb . . .
Hope that fades and thoughts that don't,
Razor cuts heal while others won't . . .
Too much despair to dare implore
The tension from beyond the door.

Pieces of me

These eyes are not mine, but they belong to me.
Without them, I know I could not see,
The smile is not mine, but it covers my face.
Without it, a frown will take its place.
Those aren't my arms that hold me tight.
Without them, I could not sleep at night.
Those aren't the lips that I use to kiss.
When you aren't here, it's me I miss.
That's not my warm breath I feel on my chest,
Or my head that lays on it to rest.
That's not my hair that's grown so long.
That's not my voice whispering that song.
I don't know where you end, or where I start.
We share a life, a soul, a heart . . .
These belong to you, but it's clear to see—
You can't leave again without taking me.

Goals

In a moment of silence and reflection,
to her, said I,
"Everyone will know my name someday."
In a moment of whimsy and intrigue
of me, asked she,
"And how, darling, will you achieve this notoriety?"
In a moment of complete lucidity
to her, replied I,
"By the horrific and grotesque way in which I depart this world."
In a moment of indifference and passive indulgence,
to me, commented she,
"Everyone should have goals."

Dark Lady

Sadness has a leverage that only she knows,
The tolerable facets of being are insufficient . . .
The only observable animation is the solemn, distant look
one attributes to the inconsolable anguish of bitter aliveness,
As the pupils behind the squinted stare dart side to side,
Reconsidering an irretrievable error in judgement
That has led to this landslide of emotional sediment,
That has buried her in the luminous rubble
of self-pity and regret
As she mindlessly twirls her coffee cup
With spindly fingers that can no longer grasp

Life of my time

for Cayce

I count not
the days, years, or breaths
of my existence . . .
The chronology is finite,
and the breaths are terminal,
But the hugs before school,
conversations about the world,
the repetitions on slides and swing sets,
conquering athletic fields,
experimenting and mastering the stuff of life,
following you through its maze,
my shadow becomes your shadow,
and the delicate kisses on your forehead
are the eternal ticking hands
of my soul.

Insomnia 2

As the phrase goes,
I am "sleeping with one eye open"
Because I cannot sleep
following our heated interchange
and because I want to be aware
of the nature and scope
of your
retribution

Stay with me

Please stay with me until my heart settles . . .
As I count the deliberate breaths and long pauses . . .
As the nimble tumbleweeds halt their carefree dance on the abandoned horizon . . .
As the breeze delicately kisses the face of the receding tide . . .
As silence earnestly seeks its seat beside honor
As the storm clouds gather for their final instrumental . . .
As anticipation and anxiety embrace their prodigal friend, peace . . .
Stay with me for the finale . . . and hold my hand . . . fingers intertwined
As I seek the truth in the promises made earlier in life
in the afterlife

Morning Coffee

They meet at the coffee maker,
Maneuvering each around the other,
Rejecting natural and artificial sweetener . . .
Eyes peer into empty cups as the steam builds
And the gurgling increases.
The aroma of discontent fills the kitchen,
Another coffee morning—
Black
Bitter

The Butterfly and the Unicorn

The butterfly hesitates on my shoulder,
Her colorful wings bending against a gentle breeze
That urges her in the direction of majestic sunrises
Surfacing from deep and far horizons . . .
The unicorn paws mindlessly at the ground,
Her prominent and majestic horn pointing toward a destiny
Of elusive and promising rainbows
Cascading from endless blue skies . . .
Me, I sit every day on the retired riverbank
Every evening, admiring the fireflies and remembering . . .
The butterfly has found greener pastures to grace,
And the unicorn is conquering further and farther rainbows

Phoenix

The phoenix will not rise,
Sometimes ashes remain ashes,
Fated ultimately to be scattered
Eternally
By the vituperative wind

The Dance

The moon on a starless night was our personal spotlight
With the timing of our steps and hearts synchronized
In the spontaneous, candid, and virtuous waltz,
My perpetual partner in passion and redemption
Elegantly gliding along life's promenade
With no choreography and no music

The Getaway

The scuffing sound of the plastic wheels
Of your suitcases across the uneven cement
Tells me the story that ends the story . . .
The cranking of your car engine is followed by
A decisive shutting of the door and
Light continued taps of uncertainty against the accelerator . . .
The hesitation in the driveway
And the slow departure of your getaway
Tell me that you will return,
Although you will never be back.

The End

She asked, "How do you know when it's finished?"
A poem, I responded, is like a relationship—
It's finished when there is nothing left
to say

The End II

"There is nothing left to say,"
She sighed

IV.

Redundant Ambiguity

Haunted Jail

What haunts us is not what we decide to do
But what we decide against
It is not the pursuit of the devil
But not chasing the angel
That leaves us misty and remorseful
The hangover of timidity
Lingers longer than the regret of intrepidness
Don't wonder in the cloud of hindsight
Be unrepentant in audacity
Don't lament the scars from the fire
Embrace the lesson from the flames
Fear of the bars of ambivalence
And the prison of hesitation

Shattered

Cuts are the price we pay
for picking up shattered pieces
It would be wiser, although unconventional, to let them lie
instead of attempting some futile resurrection
of some construct of happiness
that lies in the abstract corners of our mind
part of the illusion woven into our soul
perpetually by optimistic faux prophets
who know nothing of the heavy feeling of finally catching
and then losing the girl with the long, silken hair

Lethargy

We are afraid to charge the bending shadows
on the distant whispering hilltops
Afraid to explore the ragged darkness
of enigmatic caves we pass on the roadside
Afraid to hurdle the sagging floorboards
of anguished, abandoned. weed-tangled houses
Afraid to pursue black shrouded winter skies
of the misaligned mysterious life that follows youth

Hopscotch

In our endeavors to hopscotch and crisscross
The crippling dichotomies
Of pain and happiness
Of mourning and celebration
Of punishment and mercy
Of regret and pride
Of remorse and satisfaction
Of paucity and abundance
Of agnosticism and fervor
We exhaust ourselves with the experiences
Of being too smug and too dour

Coins

The price we pay
for faith
is the faint
innocuous splashdown
of another coin
into the fountain
of wishes

November

November is my favorite month
It does not commit to cold
It does not commit to warm
It wraps itself in the ambivalence of Autumn
With the ambiguity of sunshine and falling leaves
No promises of springtime glory, true
No isolated void of winter, in return
No adrenaline rush over new beginnings
No frozen dread that robs the warmth of our souls
November dares to remain neutral
Unresolved, equivocal, hesitant, indecisive
Never promising more than it can deliver

Change

Nothing inspires us to change like hurt
When the romance of resilience
Is replaced with the scarring of despair
We seek the shelter of idiosyncratic metamorphosis
To shield our hearts from the nefarious intentions
Of hurt that comes disguised as love and promise

A Dollar

A deposit into a slot
and the fruits of a simple action are born
there is slow, perceptible movement
industrial sounds of labor
and the purchase lingers
defiant and taunting
before surrendering to the fate of the fall
an overpriced offering from life's vending machine

Faith

I need more than a sip—
I need to dive into
and swim across the mystery
of broken sufferers who continue
to pledge allegiance to the very master
who owns the ability but lacks the compunction
to ease and abate the anguish and affliction
of those who are prostrate and convicted
and dedicated solely to a paradoxical salvation

The Judge

If you follow my dusty footprints
across an unforgiving desert
trying to retreat from your own personal prison,
you will inevitably stand before the scarlet judge
who has examined the evidence of your wasted life
for which the sentence is solitary confinement
without parole or mercy.

Hands

Our lives are shaped with our hands
and the other hands we hold
the hands of approving applause
the gesticulating hands of bitter reproach
The hands that produce the music of our lives
hands that give from one to another
hands that we hold to our faces
when we cry in the dark alone

The Candle

The whispers of a flickering candle flame
can be heard only in the silent anticipation
of the soft wavering transitioning to a violent pulse
caused by the most imperceptible movement
and darkness replaces the hope that burned
upon the wick

Grief

The grief calls to me at night . . .
My dreams are the apparitions of stolen joy.
My shadow on the wall is gripped with profound desolation . . .
The flickering candle is the funeral pyre of contentment.
The raindrops sweeping against my window are the tears of memories.
The despondent moonglow touches every corner . . .
The weeping wind moans out misery,
And I lie chilled and paralyzed, helplessly
Awaiting redemption at sunrise

Regrets

Regrets
Are dismissed premonitions
That, with a more acute awareness,
Might have been,
Instead,
Memories
Of manifested
Elation

The Path

God and I walked down a solitary dirt path.
There was silence all around,
Except for the occasional falling leaf
And crunching of dry dirt and hope under our feet.
I looked at the ground as He looked at me—
"Care for a beer?" He asked.
I shook my head without glancing up.
"Cigarette?" He inquired.
I shook my head and shrugged.
"A toke, maybe?" He inquired.
I stopped, held out my hand and asked,
"How about a prayer?"
"On no," he sighed with resignation,
"I don't do those anymore."

Happy Hour

A round of loneliness,
A few shots of despair,
A frosty mug of regret,
A mixed drink of bitter and "don't care."
Vodka with heartbreak,
Tears and a tab,
Drunk on memories,
Call me a cab.
Sorrow with a twist,
A toast to us all,
Devastation on the rocks,
This is last call

Pittsburgh

A buried heart deep in the cold mountains,
A faint pulse can be detected . . .
Beyond industrial blue steel and
The fumes of the crowded city buses
And the needy who occupy every corner,
I sat on the stone steps of the Trinity Cathedral
To watch the traffic of people who marched by . . .
And few would look and none would speak,
Even as I sat before God's temple . . .
And then the rain came and drowned all hope and anticipation . . .

Writer's Block

I cannot bear to talk anymore . . .
I cannot bear to write anymore . . .
I talk to God, and I write to you,
But the empty returns on these efforts
Leave me silent in remorse and contempt.
I have elucidated, expounded, and elaborated . . .
He cannot change your heart, and I cannot change your mind.
There is something profound in the silence.
No response, nor rejoinder, no reprimand . . .
Hours of talking and volumes of texts
Vanish into a vacuum of vanquished oratory and metaphors . . .
To lift heavy burden of indefensible indifference
And to salvage any remnant of pride and dignity,
I clear my throat and surrender my pen

Authors I know

What use is it to the world to know
every line of Edgar Allan Poe,
to recite without pause the story of the raven
while existing inconspicuously and craven?
My worldly credibility could be undercut
by exalting the merits of Vonnegut
There is some social status to be lost
Admitting wandering with Blake and Frost
Like you, my heart of been taken off track
But Emily never loved me back
I can impress the hippies with a Ginsberg quote
But the verses get buried in my throat
ee has been my companion over drinks,
Naked lunches with Burroughs' and his hijinks
I've struggled with Plath on the fringes of me
Fighting a battle of complacency
A solitary poetic neophyte
going gentle with Dylan into that good night

Silence

Silence is that flood
that drowns all hope and possibilities.
Silence is the ticking clock that marks
wasted time and counts down to regret.
Silence is the furious inferno
that turns understanding to formless ash.
Silence is the tornado
whose winds separate unity and touch.
Silence is the serial killer
that stains our memories.
Silence is the sin that strips us of our souls
and robs us of our salvation.

The Sandbox

Sandboxes are tight-knit communities
where fun and laughter are shared
and lessons learned
Today, Connor learned
that Angela does not like
her Barbie used as a javelin
and that a plastic toy shovel
is an effective weapon
of deterrence

Escorts

Grief is a ubiquitous companion
And pain is an unsolicited proxy
That accompanies us on Earth
When we are abruptly bereft
Of the defining spirits who have departed
To prematurely reserve accommodations
In the afterlife

The Kathryn Doctrine

If everyone else in the world
Would daringly feed forbidden food to the iguanas,
Cleverly hide dirty laundry beneath clean bed sheets,
Rejoice by forsaking their shoes in the wintertime,
Distinguish themselves by bouncing their kites along the ground,
Audaciously demand dominion over their father's lap,
And dauntlessly pack the suitcases of their lives with stuffed animals,
Then they, too, could experience
The free-spirited, unencumbered pleasure of undiluted happiness

Everyone is a poet

The poetry of my life has not been
The heavenly expressions or stars and rainbows
That awe observers into a coma of adoration . . .
It has not been shaped by
the uncountable blessings of time and circumstance
That bring fortunes of wealth and romance to the privileged.
It has not been impressed by
the majesty of untamed waves and currents
that provided life and legend for those submersed in them.
It has not been influenced by
the melodic laughter from parks filled with children
that provide the music of the lives of generations yielding to
generation.
It has not been guided by
the artistic expressiveness of the animal and flora
that adorn the wilderness canvas displayed by God.
It has been the result, the product, the manifestation
of those moments of disrupted harmony
that challenge each of us
to continue living.

Fountain

The fountain under which we all experience life's droplets
are but the mingling of the twin acquaintances
of recirculation and recollection.
A provisional cooling unworthy of the giggles of contentment
of the water particles misdirected temporarily toward the sky
but destined for the murky pond of uncertainty
after a truncated moment of hope and elation.

Annulment

The enchantment over the blue moon
with its mistress, the halo,
is merely the suppression of melancholy
for its jilted lover, the sun,
And the forlorn promises that
were forsaken
at dusk

The Song

We don't write the lyrics
to the songs we live.
We do not play the melody;
We do not pick the tune;
We do not control the rhythm;
We do not decide the time;
We are only the instrument
That gets played
to reflect the mood
of the Creator.

Luggage

The difference between luggage and baggage
is how they are carried.
Baggage is hoisted high
Onto the shoulders so that the weight
Can be equally bore
With the mental and emotional,
Usually unseen but obvious . . .
Baggage pulls the posture into a curved stoop
Causing the head to hang and the mind to studder.
Luggage is pulled behind
and used to whisk away and avoid
the contents of baggage

At Sunrise

Very few moments
are as gratifying,
stimulating,
creative,
and purely
exhilarating
as morning coffee
at sunrise
in my
underwear

Intermission

I rested my fingers
And pushed the stool away from the piano,
No longer able to negotiate the keys
To produce the melody one expects and appreciates
For such a long period of study, practice, and rehearsing . . .
Not forlorn, not disappointed, or regretful,
Just dispassionate, indifferent now . . .
The art is the making of the music,
The satisfaction is the product of the art . . .
And sometimes we can still love the music
Although we may longer care to play the keys . . .

Insomnia

The enticing beams from the full moon beckon me,
And the whispers from the night wind lure me.
They gesture me to the addictive shadows
Where I will forsake reason and tranquility.
The strained memories and empty echoes of laughter
Implore me to retreat to the isolated sanctuary of our bed of broken promises.
Hesitating, I drag my solitude down the stairs

Cyborg

The machine has taken over—
Steely, hard, determined . . .
Skin that is cold and industrial,
The hue of a cloudy northeastern cold front . . .
A frigid numbing sensation to the lightest touch,
Inoculated with insensitivity,
Possessing a combination of dispassion and irreverence,
Castigating mortals possessing emotion and vulnerability.
Programmed for a personal dystopia
And armed with a very prominent self-destruct button

The Couch

The couch is the ultimate companion to silence . . .
Its cushions are stuffed fully with resentment,
It is the coffin of understanding and empathy,
And the final resting place of compromise and caring . . .
It is the manifest statement to surrender and indifference . . .
The wasteland sought early in the evening
For the extended hibernation
Of what was once disguised as love.

Soulmates

Love is when
two people prefer the
volatility, combustibility,
conflict, and disruption
of togetherness
Over the predictable
tranquility and unabated
serenity of
the personal dominion
of autonomy

The Fortress

The rain that you are experiencing
will drench and soften
and peel away
the walls of the box
in which you have barricaded
yourself,
And provide you
the freedom
of a liberated soul
and a life
still flush
with possibilities.

The Sword

Love is like a sword . . .
True, there is finality of any wound,
but the edge will cut
layer from layer,
slice after slice . . .
a deepening wound—
fatal upon the removal
of the protections of ego and pride . . .
But with the tip,
a thrust that finds its mark
will find the heart
and quickly remove the soul,
leaving no time for reflection
or regret . . .
Just mercy.

Reapers

Death and I strolled aimlessly
One late fall day,
Wandering over rolling acres of untamed wilderness,
randomly picking and blowing away dandelion buds,
probing the grass for 4-leaf clovers,
practicing quiet introspection,
and sending occasional glances at the gathering clouds . . .
After that extended silence,
An observation was offered—
"It must be very wearisome being the reaper.
The mere anticipation of you can paralyze anyone.
Everything you touch immediately expires,
Eternally delivering death and despondency,
Being the personification of fear and dread,
The subject of nightmares,
The embodiment of an unavoidable and unwelcomed fate,
The personal narrative of terror,
A solitary loathsome and despised figure,
The messenger of grief and escort to the crypt,
An enduring legend of misery
Reviled in the universe and eternity . . ."
"You learn to live with it,"
I said.

Dancing Scarecrow

A scarecrow can only dance when assisted by an obliging wind.
When his ragged and patched overalls lift and flail
for the entertainment of the black crows and field mice,
It is at the pleasure of the autumn wind
When the scarecrow's tattered straw hat
reaches for the sky and circles his pillowcase head
and orbits his body, tethered only by its cotton string,
It is the whimsy of the gusts mocking the marionette.
When the scarecrow's checkered shirt puffs in pride
And raises the insubstantial sleeves in rebellion,
it is the force of a zephyr that can be applied and withdrawn
at God's singular discretion,
Reminding us that we are all scarecrows

The Book of Me

The book of me is incomplete,
an unpaginated epic narrative
where the weight of satisfaction
is only slightly heavier than that of regret . . .
Pages and pages, chapter after chapter,
about an anonymous protagonist
whose conflicts are perpetuated by his ambivalent
relationship with God.
There are scattered footnotes
to help you read between the lines,
which have been blurred over time by the
competing antagonists of indifference and passion.
In the final pages, you may wonder
if it was biography or fiction,
and that would be accurate.

Currents

As the tide of my life
Washes towards an uncertain horizon,
I will drift away secure in the fact
That my life was best lived through you,
And eternity can have me
As unequal compensation

The House Across the Street

The lethargic siding, wilting columns,
and surrendering shingles
invited the serpentine vines, menacing limbs,
and ambitious weeds
to methodically and emphatically
strangle the windows
and suffocate the doorways.
The lights have long diminished,
and the wind whistles through the empty rafters.
Forsaken by ghosts and abandoned by memories,
Its shell is dusted by a quilt
of pollen and dandelion tears.

Aspirations

It is the raging current of conceptual celebrity
That propels unseasoned souls
Toward the delusive pursuit of elusory rainbows
And compels them with the nonsensical notion
Of domesticating exalted unicorns . . .
The futility of the superficial pursuits
Fractures spirits and undermines conviction,
While pragmatism and a passion,
Predicated on the preference for anonymity,
Prevents the skeptic from the predestination
Of a profound and terminal bashing
From a territorial leprechaun . . .
Or being impaled on the pronounced horn
Of a disobliging unicorn.

Baptism

"Finally, I can be," I exclaimed,
As the rain soaked my clothes and returned my lucidity . . .
And I fell upon the muddy bank of a nearby pond,
Kicking merrily and defiantly toward the scurrying black clouds,
Shouting incoherently at the prying geese and the inquisitive turtles,
Disrobing myself to fully experience the pitch marshmallow beneath my back and the unmistakable emersion of my body into earth . . .
I laughed at those furies and deprived them of their conceived punishments,
Clinching my own destiny and choking away the life
From the sins impressed upon me by misplaced trust and defective cognition . . .
Hysterically mocking the flamingos as I lay bare to the elements,
Embracing the raw, bestial expressions from this climacteric baptism . . .
Inevitably, the forlorn sun broke through and illuminated the restraints of awareness and conformity
To a broken soul and despairing spirit.

"Woke" Barbie

The label read:
"If you buy this white
toxic
stereotype
for your female
child,
you are a
bigoted,
homophobic,
classist,
racist,
oppressive
misogynist"
(Made in China)

Facebook

Shadows and echoes
and wandering souls
believe that
Dignity may be imported,
Esteem can be contrived,
Value can be gained from unseen masses . . .
An elusive pursuit of validation
through conformity
following those who follow
the piper . . .

Jack-in-the-box

We slowly, dutifully
Turn the handle of life,
One eye open
For anticipated surprises,
On edge,
Waiting for the jack-in-the-box
Of our efforts,
Only to conclude
That the lid
Has been sealed all along,
And our turning and expectations
Have revealed a different sort of clown

Where do I go?

Where do I go now?
Futilely clinging to a broken compass
whose arrows alternate between a capricious nowhere
and a undetermined somewhere . . .
Standing at the crossroads of anonymity
and an enduring legacy . . .
Exposed, digging my toes into the mud of uncertainty

About the Author

Dr. Michael Roberts is Professor of English, teaching college and university courses that include Introduction to Literature, Literary Criticism, US. Authors post-1865, and lectures that include Harlem Renaissance Poetry, Modernism, and Beat Poetry.

He has a Doctoral degree from N.C. State University, a M.A. from UNC Pembroke, and a B.A. from St. Andrews University. He has taught at the college level for over 20 years.

Scribbled Lines: Life in Pieces is his first full collection of poetry. He has published two chapbook collections entitled *Random Roadside Cemetery* and *Daughters, Soulmates, and the Spirit in the Urn*. He has also published research books and articles on education and curriculum development.

Dr. Roberts is the father of two daughters, Cayce and Kathryn, who he cites as the original inspirations for his creative writing.

He currently resides quietly on the Waccamaw River in Conway, SC, with his wife, Angela, and puppy, Sheldon, where he spends his time fishing, writing, and trying to keep death at bay.

www.ingramcontent.com/pod-product-compliance
Lightning Source LLC
Chambersburg PA
CBHW060837190426
43197CB00040B/2669